The Trojan Horse
and other Greek Myths and Legends

Retold by Linda Strachan

Contents

Section 1

Persephone and the Coming of Winter	2
The Trojan Horse	6

Section 2

Perseus and Medusa	12
Theseus and the Minotaur	17

Section 3

Jason and the Golden Fleece	22
Odysseus and the Cyclops	27
Appendix – Greek and Roman Names	32

Edinburgh Gate
Harlow, Essex

Persephone and the Coming of Winter (Per-sef-o-nay)

Have you ever wondered why we have different seasons during the year? The ancient Greeks blamed the Gods for everything that happened on Earth. The story of Persephone explained why all the plants and flowers died in the winter and grew back again in the spring.

Persephone was very beautiful. Her mother, Demeter, was the Goddess of Nature and she made all the plants, flowers and harvests grow and ripen.

One day, when Persephone was out with her friends, Hades, the God of the Underworld, saw her and fell in love with her. Hades went to see his brother, Zeus. Zeus was the King of all the Gods and he ruled from Mount Olympus.

"I have seen a beautiful girl," Hades told Zeus. "I want to marry her."

Zeus knew that Demeter would never let her daughter marry Hades because the Underworld was the Land of the Dead. It was a gloomy place with no colour or sunshine. So Zeus didn't give his brother a proper answer.

"I don't think it would be a good idea," Zeus told Hades.

The next day, Hades found Persephone all by herself, picking flowers in her garden.

"Zeus didn't say I *couldn't* marry her," he thought to himself. So Hades grabbed Persephone and whisked her away to the Underworld in his chariot.

When Demeter found out that her daughter was missing she searched all over the world for her. She was miserable because she didn't know what had become of her beautiful daughter. The search took a very long time and, while she was searching, Demeter forgot about the plants and flowers that grew on the Earth. Without Demeter to look after them, the harvests failed and all the plants on Earth died.

When Zeus saw this he called Demeter up to Mount Olympus, the home of the gods.

"What has happened, Demeter?" Zeus asked her. "Why are all the plants dying?"

"Persephone has disappeared," Demeter told him. "I can do nothing else until I find her."

Zeus knew that without the harvests the mortals on Earth would have nothing to eat and they would die. He wondered if Hades knew where Persephone was, so he went down to the Underworld to find Hades.

Hades did not want Persephone to leave him. Zeus told him that he could not allow all the mortals on Earth to starve to death. Hades argued with Zeus but in the end he agreed that Persephone could return to her mother. Zeus said everything would be fine as long as Persephone had not eaten any of the food of the Underworld.

Persephone was sad at being away from her mother and her friends and all the flowers she loved so much. She had been so unhappy that she had not eaten anything at all. But, just before she was due to leave, Hades persuaded her to eat some seeds from a pomegranate.

When Zeus heard this he called Persephone to Mount Olympus. "Since you have eaten the food of the Underworld you cannot leave it. You must stay with Hades."

Persephone listened quietly but tears gathered in her eyes. "Can I no longer go home?" she asked. "What of the mortals who are starving? What of my mother, Demeter, whose heart is breaking?"

Zeus, who was very wise, stroked his long beard thoughtfully for a few moments.

"I have decided," he said. "You will live one third of the year in the Underworld with Hades and for the rest of the year you may live on Earth with your mother, Demeter."

So Persephone lived on Earth with her mother for two thirds of the year. During that time the plants and flowers and all the harvests flourished. When the time came for her to leave Earth and go down to the Underworld, Demeter was so sad to see her daughter go that all the plants died.

The ancient Greeks believed that during winter all plants died because Persephone lived in the Underworld with Hades. In the spring when they began to grow and blossom again it was because Persephone had returned to Earth to be with her mother for the rest of the year.

The Trojan Horse

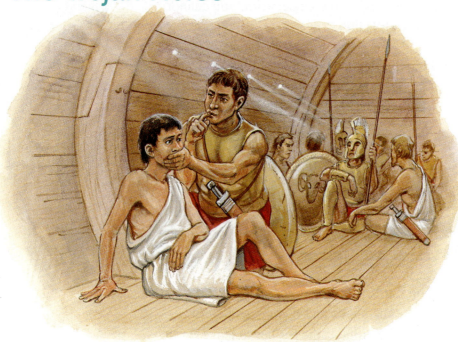

My name is Lo, short for Loniceus. My brother and I are part of the Greek army and we are camped outside the city of Troy. I look older than my years but I only got to join the army by pestering my father so much that he made my older brother take me along.

Yesterday I climbed into the belly of the great wooden horse which the carpenters have been making for the last month. No-one would tell me why the horse was so big, or why they were lifting a water barrel into the huge empty space inside. I found a small trapdoor and climbed in when no-one was looking. But it got so hot that I fell asleep and when I woke up the horse was being moved.

I was about to shout and tell them I was inside, when a hand covered my mouth.

"Shhh, Lo!" It was my brother, Granos. When I looked around I saw that there were many other warriors in the belly of the horse, even Odysseus himself. They were not making a sound but I could feel the horse sway as it was pulled over the rough ground.

"What's going on?" I asked my brother in a whisper.

"We are going to invade Troy, little brother." He spoke just loud enough for me to hear him above the rumble of the wheels. I saw Odysseus glance at him.

Granos showed me a crack in the side of the horse. I could see that we were now far from our own camp, almost at the walls of the city of Troy. We have been at war with Troy for years – ever since Paris ran off with Helen and took her back to Troy with him.

Helen is said to be the most beautiful woman that ever lived. Menelaus, the King of Sparta, is her husband. When he realised that she had gone he got all the other Greek princes to help him bring her back.

Although we Greeks are great warriors we have not yet managed to win the war. I wondered how this small group of warriors were going to do what all the Greek army had not been able to do. I looked through the crack between the wooden planks of the horse. All of our ships were already sailing away from Troy. I pointed them out to Granos.

"They are leaving us!" I told him. I was beginning to feel really scared. I had heard what the Trojans do to their prisoners.
"Don't worry, Lo," Granos whispered. "Odysseus has a great plan."

Granos told me that the wooden horse would be left outside the city as an offering to the goddess Athene. The Trojans would take the horse into the city and we would open the gates.

"But our ships are leaving!" I whispered.
"They will be back when they get the signal," Granos told me. "But be quiet now because the Trojans must think the horse is empty."

The rumbling stopped and I heard shouts as the ropes that had been used to pull the horse were taken off. Odysseus looked around at all of us, warning us to keep quiet.

It was a long time before anything happened. Everyone rested as much as they could. Some bread and a bottle of water was passed around when it got really hot during the day. I was so hungry I could have eaten anything, but the bread and water helped a bit.

Suddenly I heard someone shouting. The horse began to move again. It swayed so much that I thought it was about to fall over. The barrel of water rocked but Odysseus grabbed it, and he and two others held it steady. If it had fallen over, the Trojans would have wondered why a wooden offering to Athene was dripping water!

Through the crack I could see the great gates of Troy as we passed through them and on into the city. I was both excited and scared.

That night the Trojans started to celebrate because they had seen our ships sailing off. Granos told me that Sinon, one of our warriors, had let himself be caught by the Trojans! Sinon was going to tell them that he had escaped from Odysseus who did not like him. He was to say that Odysseus wanted to kill him and offer him to the Gods so that the ships would have a good wind to sail by. Sinon was to tell the Trojans that the Greeks had decided to go home and the wooden horse was an offering to the goddess Athene for a safe journey on the sea.

I know Sinon, I have watched him play dice with my brother and I didn't think he was anyone special. But I think he must be very brave to let the Trojans catch him. What if they don't believe him? Even if they do, they might still kill him.

During the Trojans' celebration Sinon was to light a fire to tell our ships that the plan had worked and we would be opening the gates of Troy for the Greek army.

It was quite late when Sinon came and opened the trapdoor in the horse. The warriors all climbed out, but I was told to stay in the horse until Troy had fallen.

I watched them all leave but I didn't want to hide. So when everyone had gone I crept out of the horse and went towards the gates of the city. The air was filled with the sound of fighting. I could see that our army had returned and the war with Troy was almost over.

The fighting was exciting to watch but one or two things I saw were so horrible that I was in a corner being sick when Granos found me. He just laughed, and told me that I will become a great warrior when I grow up, with a stronger stomach. I hope so!

Perseus and Medusa

When Perseus was a young man King Polydectes decided that he wanted to marry Danae, Perseus' mother. Danae didn't like Polydectes and she refused him. Polydectes decided that if he could get rid of her son, Perseus, he would have better luck with Danae. He needed to find a way to get rid of Perseus.

"I will have a great banquet," he told his nobles. "All my subjects are invited and they must each bring me a present."

At the banquet all the nobles brought the King presents. The King saw Perseus. "And what have you brought me, young Perseus?"

"I am a poor man. I have nothing to bring you," Perseus replied.

The King thumped the arm of his throne. "After all the kindness we have shown you and your mother, is this the way you repay us? Have you not even a horse you could give as a present to your King?"

Perseus shook his head. "I could as easily bring you the head of Medusa the Gorgon," he said, in jest.

King Polydectes saw at once that this was the way to get rid of the boy for good.

"And so you shall, Perseus. You shall bring me the head of Medusa." With a sly smile Polydectes listened to the gasps of horror. "Or are you also lacking in courage?" he asked.

Perseus only hesitated for a moment. "I shall bring you the head of Medusa the Gorgon," he said.

The Gorgons were three sisters who had claws of bronze and golden wings. Instead of hair, their heads were covered in snakes. Medusa was the only one who was mortal and could be killed, but one look was all she needed to turn you to stone.

As he left the palace, Perseus met a beautiful woman and a young man. The woman was the goddess Athene who had decided to help him.

"So you think you can cut off Medusa's head before she turns you into stone, Perseus?" Athene asked him.

Perseus stood with his head held high. "I can try," he said.

The Goddess held out a shield and a leather bag. "Take this shining shield. When you enter her cave use it as a mirror so that you do not look at Medusa. The bag is for her head so that you may carry it safely."

"What will you use to cut off her head?" asked the young man. When Perseus showed him his knife the young man laughed. He stepped up into the air. He was wearing winged sandals and at once Perseus recognised him as Hermes, the messenger of the Gods.

A scythe appeared in Perseus' hands. It was long and incredibly sharp.

"Use that to cut off her head," Hermes told him. "My sandals will allow you to enter her cave without Medusa hearing you."

Perseus looked down and found that Hermes' winged sandals were now on his feet.

"One other thing, brave Perseus," Athene said, softly. "You must go to the Nymphs and borrow the Cap of Invisibility that belongs to the God Hades."

"Where will I find the Nymphs?" asked Perseus.

Hermes looked down at him. "Go and ask the Three Grey Sisters," he said.

The Three Grey Sisters lived far away, but the magic sandals lifted Perseus into the air and soon he was heading across the sea, far away from Greece.

The Three Grey Sisters were old crones with only one eye and one tooth between them. When Perseus approached they were sitting, screeching at each other.

"Good day to you, Sisters," he said, politely.

"Who is it?" screamed one of the sisters. She grabbed the eye and peered at him through it. "What do you want?"

"I am Perseus," he began, "Athene said that I might ask you where to find the Nymphs."

"Let me see him!" squealed the second sister. She scowled at Perseus. "No, we don't want to tell you. Go away!"

"Give me the eye, it's my turn!" The third sister tried to grab the eye but Perseus stepped into the air and snatched the eye from her. He floated above them. "Now tell me where the Nymphs live and you may have your eye back."

The Sisters cursed and moaned but they told him where to find the Nymphs. Perseus dropped the eye on the beach and left them to fight over it.

The Nymphs lived beside a huge mountain which reached up into the clouds. When Perseus got there he found Atlas holding up the sky. Atlas wondered if Perseus had stolen Hermes' sandals but when Perseus told him his story, Atlas called the Nymphs. He told them to give Perseus the Cap of Invisibility. With a promise to return it, Perseus left for the lair of the Gorgons.

When he reached the shore where the Gorgons lived, Perseus saw the shapes of all the poor men and creatures that had been turned to stone by a look from Medusa.

Using his enchanted shield as a mirror, he looked into the cave and saw that the Gorgons were sleeping. He put on Hades' cap which turned him invisible and flew silently towards them. He saw Medusa reflected in the shield. Her head of snakes hissed even as she slept. With one swipe of the scythe he chopped off her head and thrust it into his bag. Perseus flew swiftly out of the cave before her sisters woke up.

After stopping to return Hades' cap to the Nymphs, Perseus made his way home. When he got there he discovered that Polydectes had imprisoned Danae until she agreed to marry him.

Perseus went to the King who was amazed to see him again.

"So you came back, Perseus! Was Medusa too frightening after all?" Polydectes and all his nobles laughed.

"No!" said Perseus as he opened his bag and closed his eyes. He held up Medusa's head. "Here she is!" he said. But there was no sound at all because Polydectes and all his nobles had been turned to stone.

Theseus and the Minotaur

Can you imagine an enormous beast with the head of a bull and the body of a man? That was what the Minotaur looked like. Below Knossos, the great palace of King Minos of Crete, was the Labyrinth, a maze of tunnels. The Minotaur lived in the Labyrinth.

When his son was killed in Athens, King Minos demanded compensation for his loss. So, every nine years, fourteen young men and women from Athens were sent to Crete to be eaten by the Minotaur. The fourteen young men and women were chosen by drawing names out of a pot.

Aegeus was King of Athens, and his son Theseus, who was also the son of the god Poseidon, was the heir to his throne. Theseus was a brave young man and he put his name into the pot without telling his father. Theseus was the last name drawn out of the pot and when he saw it King Aegeus turned very pale.

"There must be some mistake!" he cried.

"No, Father, there is no mistake," Theseus replied. "I will go to Crete and I shall kill the Minotaur so that no more of our people will be fed to that monster."

With a heavy heart King Aegeus watched the ship prepare to set sail for Crete. At the last moment he grabbed the captain by the arm.

"If Theseus is still alive when you return, fly white sails from the masts so that I will know he is safe," the King said. "If I see black sails I will know that my son is dead."

"You worry too much, Father," the young man laughed. "When I return the ship will have white sails and all Athens will celebrate!"

When they arrived at the shores of Crete, King Minos was waiting. He had heard that King Aegeus had sent his son, Theseus.

"Where is Theseus?" King Minos asked.

"I am Theseus, son of Poseidon. I have come to kill the Minotaur."

King Minos laughed. "You are a boastful young man. Perhaps you should prove your heritage. If you are indeed the son of Poseidon then you will be able to bring back this ring!" With a jerk of his hand, King Minos threw his gold ring far into the sea. "Bring back the ring or you will die here, before you even glimpse the Minotaur!"

Theseus dived into the water and asked his father, Poseidon, for help.

Poseidon heard him and sent the Nereids, sea goddesses, to find the ring. When Theseus emerged from the sea with the ring in his hand, everyone, except King Minos, was delighted.

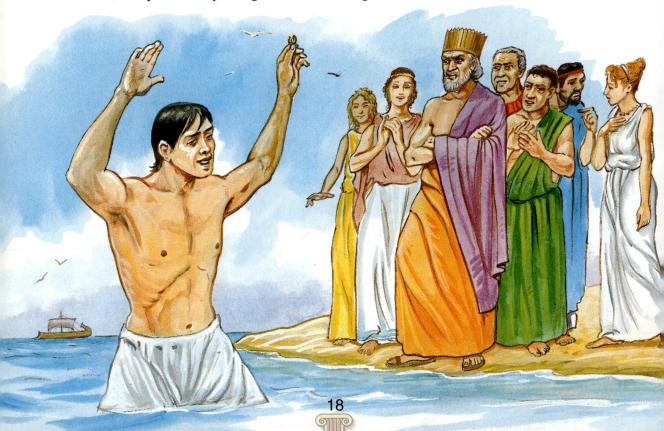

"You shall be the first to meet the Minotaur," King Minos told Theseus. "Then we shall see how brave you are!"

King Minos had a beautiful daughter called Ariadne. That night she went to see Theseus in his prison cell.

"I can help you defeat the Minotaur," she whispered.

"How can you help me?" asked Theseus.

Ariadne showed him a ball of twine. "Tie this to the entrance of the Labyrinth and it will lead you to the Minotaur. When you have killed it, you can follow the twine and it will show you the way out of the Labyrinth."

Theseus took the twine. "Thank you, Ariadne, but why are you doing this?"

"Promise that you will take me back to Athens as your wife when you have killed the Minotaur," she asked him.

"Very well," Theseus nodded. "I will."

Ariadne slipped away just before the guards arrived to take Theseus to the Labyrinth.

The Labyrinth was a huge maze with hundreds of tunnels. No-one who entered it had ever come out alive. If the Minotaur did not eat them they got lost and starved to death. Theseus tied the twine to a rock at the entrance. When he laid it down it began to roll along the ground. Theseus followed it until he reached the Minotaur's lair. The Minotaur was incredibly strong but Theseus gave a bloodcurdling war cry and ran to meet it. Theseus fought the Minotaur and at last he managed to kill it.

Although Theseus was tired he didn't stop to rest. He followed the twine back out of the Labyrinth and went straight to the prison and freed the young men and women of Athens.

"You are free!" he told them. "The Minotaur is dead!"

They fled quickly to their ship because no-one knew what King Minos would do when he found out that the Minotaur had been killed.

Ariadne was waiting by the ship. She was delighted to see that Theseus was unharmed. Theseus helped her onto the ship and they set sail for Athens.

On the way home they stopped at the island of Naxos to collect water. Ariadne was tired as she had not slept at all the night before. Theseus suggested she should rest on the island, where it was quiet.

When they were ready to leave, Theseus saw that Ariadne was still sleeping and decided to leave her behind. He did not want to marry her, and forgot that she had been the one who had helped him to find his way through the Labyrinth.

When she woke up alone, Ariadne called to the gods for revenge on Theseus for forgetting his promise and abandoning her. The god Dionysus was passing by and when he saw Ariadne he fell in love with her. Ariadne still wanted her revenge, so Dionysus made Theseus so happy to be going home that he forgot all about changing the sails on his ship from black to white. When they approached Athens with black sails, King Aegeus, watching from the clifftop, believed that his son Theseus had been killed by the Minotaur.

He was so sad that he threw himself over the cliffs and drowned in the sea. The sea where King Aegeus drowned was named the Aegean Sea and it is still called that today.

Jason and the Golden Fleece

Jason should have been heir to the throne of Iolcus but his father had lost his kingdom to his brother, Pelias. Cheated of his inheritance by his uncle, Jason grew up in exile.

On his way back to Iolcus to claim his throne, he helped an old woman cross a stream and, in the process, lost one of his sandals. This might seem like an unimportant detail but King Pelias, Jason's uncle, had been told by the Oracle* that a one-sandalled man would take his throne from him. When he saw Jason arrive with only one sandal he was worried and told Jason that if he wanted the throne he would have to prove himself by bringing back the Golden Fleece.

The Golden Fleece was kept in a sacred grove and protected by a fire-breathing dragon. No-one had ever succeeded in getting past the dragon but Jason was determined that he would accomplish the task. He gathered together as many brave warriors as he could find and asked them to accompany him.

Amongst them was Argus, a skilled carpenter, who built their ship which they named the *Argo*. Those who sailed with Jason became known as the Argonauts.

Heracles, renowned for his great strength, was one of these warriors, along with Orpheus who was skilled in playing the lyre. Lynceus, whose sharp eyes could see farther than anyone else, even through stone walls, was the look-out. Tiphys could read the stars like a map, so he was to be their navigator. The only woman among them was Atalanta. No-one could match her skills with bow and arrow.

*Oracle

When the gods wanted to communicate with mortals, or mortals had a question they wanted to ask the gods, they consulted the Oracle.

But the messages were often a bit muddled, like when you have your fortune told. Sometimes the messages were misunderstood.

There were many other heroes on the *Argo* and they had several adventures on their way to Colchis, where the Golden Fleece was to be found.

Finally they arrived, but King Aietes had no intention of letting Jason take his Golden Fleece. He realised that Jason and the Argonauts did not want to leave without it, so he set Jason three almost impossible tasks.

"If you can complete these tasks you may keep the Golden Fleece," the King announced.

"What are these tasks?" Jason asked him.

"First, you must harness my two fire-breathing bulls and plough the Field of Mars. Then, you must plant dragon's teeth in the field, and finally you must take the Golden Fleece from the tree that is guarded by my dragon."

Jason agreed to meet King Aietes the next morning at the Field of Mars, which was just outside the city. He hoped the Gods would help him succeed in these challenges.

That night, the King's daughter, Medea, came to see Jason. She had fallen in love with him and, as she was an enchantress and knew all about spells, she gave Jason a potion to rub all over himself before he went to harness the bulls.

"This will make you invulnerable so that the fire from the bulls' breath will not harm you," she said.

"I thank you for this, Medea, but can you tell me what will happen when I plant the dragon's teeth in the field?" Jason asked her.

Medea shivered. "Giants will spring from the Earth where the teeth are planted. They will try to kill you. They are very bad tempered, but if you throw a couple of stones at the ones in the middle you will be safe."

The next morning Jason rubbed on the magic potion Medea had given him. When he went to harness the bulls their breath of fire felt cool on his skin and did not burn him. He ploughed the field and started to plant the dragon's teeth. They sank into the ground as he dropped them.

Within a few moments giant warriors erupted from the soft brown soil and came towards Jason. They looked fierce and angry. Jason remembered what Medea had said. He picked up a couple of stones and tossed them into the middle of the crowd of giants.

He heard the stones hit one of the giants and within moments they were squabbling amongst themselves, accusing each other of throwing stones. Jason watched as the giants began to fight, knocking each other down until there were none left standing in the field.

King Aietes was angry when he saw that Jason had managed to survive his first two challenges. He told Jason that he should not attempt the next challenge until the following morning.

Jason and his men were resting when Medea came to them.

"My father does not intend to let you try to take the Golden Fleece from the tree. He is preparing his soldiers to come to kill you all tonight."

"We must go and get the Golden Fleece now," said Jason. "Before King Aietes is ready."

"I will come with you," Medea said. "Orpheus should come, too. He should bring his lyre."

As Medea had already saved him twice, Jason decided to do as she asked. He and Orpheus followed Medea to the sacred grove where the dragon guarded the Golden Fleece.

"The dragon is immortal," Medea whispered, as they approached it. "It cannot be killed."

"How are we to get the fleece?" asked Jason.

"Orpheus, play your sweetest tune," Medea commanded.

Orpheus began to play and the dragon started to move gently to the music. Within moments it had fallen asleep.

"Quickly, Jason," said Medea. "It will not last for very long."

Jason climbed the tree and lifted down the heavy fleece which was made of pure gold. He and Orpheus carried it back to the *Argo* which was ready to sail. Jason, Orpheus and Medea got on board with the Golden Fleece and the ship set sail. King Aietes and his army arrived at the shore. He was furious, but unable to stop them.

When Jason returned to Iolcus with the Golden Fleece, King Pelias was angry that Jason had succeeded, but he was forced to give up his throne. Soon afterwards, Jason became King.

Odysseus and the Cyclops

On their return voyage after the siege of Troy, Odysseus and his fleet of ships were blown off course by a fierce gale. They sought shelter in a group of islands in the land of the Cyclopes.

Since they needed provisions, Odysseus chose twelve of his men to accompany him in one of the smaller ships. They headed towards one of the islands. They took casks of wine which was so strong that it had to be diluted twelve times to make it safe to drink. It was wonderful wine and Odysseus thought it would be fine to use in exchange for the provisions they needed.

The island had an enormous cave on it. Outside the cave there were goats and sheep grazing.

Odysseus and his men went into the cave. They were surprised to find that it was stacked with fine cheeses and pots of milk from the goats. The owner of this fine produce could not be found, so Odysseus and his men helped themselves to some cheese and milk while they waited.

Just before dark the goats and sheep were herded into the cave. Behind them was a Cyclops, a huge creature the size of three men. It had one large eye in the middle of its forehead. Odysseus and his men were stunned into silence as the fearsome creature came into the cave.

As soon as the animals were safely inside, the Cyclops lifted an enormous stone and placed it over the entrance to the cave.

"Strangers!" exclaimed the Cyclops, when he saw the men in his cave. "Who are you? Are you pirates come to steal what you can?"

"We are sailors, stranded on these islands by a fierce storm," Odysseus told him. "We hope you will supply us with food to help us reach home safely. We are happy to trade with you."

"I care not for strangers who come to my cave and help themselves to my food."

With one swipe the Cyclops swept two of the men into the air and, to the horror of those watching, he threw them against the wall and then he sat down and ate them.

When he finished his meal the Cyclops lay down on the floor and fell sound asleep.

Odysseus wanted to kill the monster but he realised that he and his men could not push the giant stone away from the entrance to the cave. He would have to think of some way to make the Cyclops move the stone, so that they could escape.

The next morning the Cyclops ate another two of Odysseus' men. After his meal, the monster opened the cave and chased the sheep and goats outside but, offering no chance of escape, he quickly put the stone back and sealed Odysseus and his men inside.

While they waited for the Cyclops to return, Odysseus planned their escape. He ordered the men to sharpen the end of a large wooden pole, which was almost as large as the main mast of their ship, and to lay it in the ashes of the fire until it was hot.

When the Cyclops returned for the night, he closed the stone over the entrance once more. He ate another two of the men and, as he was about to lie down, Odysseus called to him.

"Cyclops, do you not want some wine to drink after your meal? I have some wonderful wine for you."

The Cyclops tasted the strong wine that Odysseus had brought with him.

"This is indeed wonderful wine," the Cyclops said, helping himself to another cask. "Tell me, what is your name?"

The wine was not diluted at all and with every cask of wine he drank the Cyclops became more drunk.

"You asked my name?" Odysseus answered the Cyclops. "I am called Nobody."

"Well, Nobody, my name is Polyphemus," said the Cyclops. "This is very good wine!" With that, he fell sound asleep on the floor of the cave.

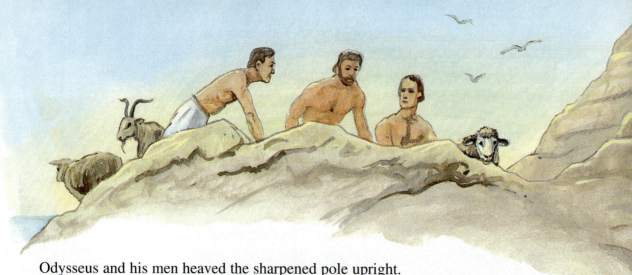

Odysseus and his men heaved the sharpened pole upright.
They lifted it and plunged it into the Cyclops' single eye.
The creature moaned and cried out in pain, but he was blinded.

When the other Cyclopes heard his cries, they arrived outside the cave and shouted. "What is wrong, Polyphemus? Is someone stealing your goats and sheep? Is someone hurting you?"

"Help," moaned Polyphemus, "Nobody is hurting me!"
he told them.

"Then stop all your noise and let us sleep!" said the other Cyclopes.

In the morning Polyphemus opened the cave and stood at the entrance to let his sheep and goats out. Because he could not see, he felt the top of each one to make sure it was a sheep or goat and not one of the treacherous men. He was not about to let them escape.

What Polyphemus did not know was that during the night Odysseus and his men had tied the sheep together in threes. One of the men was strapped under the stomach of the middle sheep of each group.

When all his men had passed Polyphemus safely, Odysseus climbed under the ram which was the biggest of all the sheep. He held on tightly to its thick curly coat as he passed Polyphemus.

"Why are you out last, my favourite ram?" muttered Polyphemus. "Usually you are the first out of the cave. You must be sad for the treatment I have received from Nobody. I will not let him get away with this terrible deed."

As soon as they escaped from the cave, Odysseus and his men dropped to the ground and herded all the sheep and the goats towards their ship.

They set sail as fast as they could and soon reached the island where the rest of the fleet were waiting. Before long they were heading towards home with plenty of sheep and goats to give them milk, cheese and meat for the rest of their journey.

Appendix – Greek and Roman Names

Often the Greeks and the Romans had different names for the same characters or Gods in their stories. Sometimes it was only the spelling that was different.

Story page number	Greek name	Roman name
2	Persephone	Proserpina
2	Demeter	Ceres
2	Hades	Pluto
6, 27	Odysseus	Ulysses
13	Athene	Minerva
13	Hermes	Mercury
17	Poseidon	Neptune
21	Dionysus	Bacchus
22	Heracles	Hercules